The MAILBOX® The Education Center®

grade

W9-DDY-755

Phenomenal Phonics®

Phonics Games

Reproducible Lotto Games for Reinforcing

- **Long Vowels**
- **Diphthongs**
- **Three-Letter Blends**
- **Contractions**

Managing Editor: Gerri Primak

Editorial Team: Becky S. Andrews, Kimberley Bruck, Karen P. Shelton, Diane Badden, Thad H. McLaurin, Sharon Murphy, Lynn Drolet, Kelly Robertson, Karen A. Brudnak, Juli Docimo Blair, Hope Rodgers, Dorothy C. McKinney

Production Team: Lori Z. Henry, Pam Crane, Rebecca Saunders, Jennifer Tipton Cappoen, Chris Curry, Sarah Foreman, Theresa Lewis Goode, Greg D. Rieves, Eliseo De Jesus Santos II, Barry Slate, Donna K. Teal, Zane Williard, Tazmen Carlisle, Kathy Coop, Marsha Heim, Lynette Dickerson, Mark Rainey

Reproducible Assessments Also Included!

www.themailbox.com

©2007 The Mailbox®
All rights reserved.
ISBN10 #1-56234-749-7 • ISBN13 #978-156234-749-9

Manufactured in the United States
10 9 8 7 6 5 4 3 2 1

Table of Contents

Lotto Games

Assessments

What's Inside

Phonics Games contains ten reproducible lotto games, each reinforcing a different skill. Each game includes the following:

- directions for the teacher
- six different reproducible gameboards
- reproducible teacher cards
- a reproducible follow-up assessment page

Teacher Directions

Gameboards

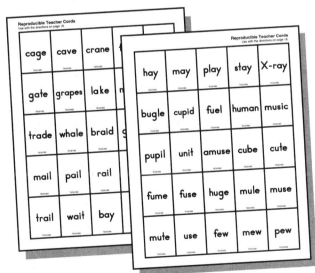

Teacher Cards

Assessment Page

Also Included:
- assessment pages to review long vowels and diphthongs
- reproducible student brag tags
- reproducible storage labels

Brag Tags
Copy onto colorful construction paper, cut out, and use as rewards for each game.

Copy onto colorful construction paper, cut out, and use as rewards for each game.

©The Mailbox® • *Phenomenal Phonics*® *Games* • TEC61063

More Cheese, Please!
Long a and Long e Game

Directions:

What you need:

- gameboard copy (pages 7–9) for each player

- game markers, such as ¾" construction paper squares

- copy of the reproducible teacher cards (pages 10 and 11), cut apart, shuffled, and placed in an envelope

1. Give game markers and a gameboard to each child. Have her read each word and name each picture on her board, noting the different spellings of long /a/ and long /e/. Provide assistance as necessary.

2. Explain that when a student hears a word that is written or pictured on her board, she is to cover it with a marker.

3. Describe the criteria for winning: four in a row (vertically, horizontally, or diagonally) or four corners. Ask that winners say, "More cheese, please!" to signal their wins.

4. To play, remove a card from the envelope and read it aloud. (As you use the cards, place them faceup in alphabetical order for your later reference.) Students who have the matching word or picture cover it.

5. Play continues until someone calls out, "More cheese, please!" To verify her win, have her uncover and read or name each word or picture as you check her responses. For an added challenge, have her spell any pictured word that she uncovers.

See page 66 for a student assessment page.

More Cheese, Please!
Long a and Long e Game

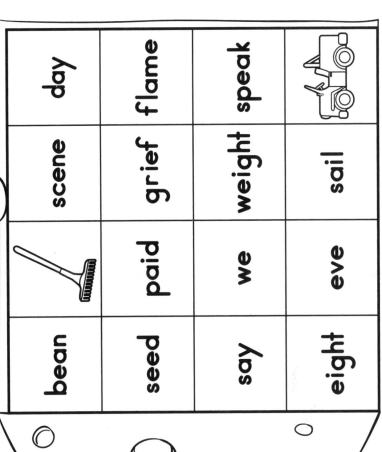

day	scene		bean
flame	grief	paid	seed
speak	weight	we	say
	sail	eve	eight

More Cheese, Please!
Long a and Long e Game

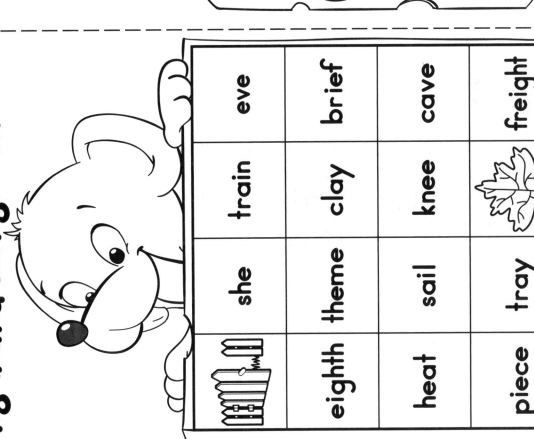

eve	train	she	
brief	clay	theme	eighth
cave	knee	sail	heat
freight		tray	piece

7

More Cheese, Please!
Long a and Long e Game

play	maze		field
nail	he	sleigh	bean
knee		thief	eighth
weed	scene	paint	shade

More Cheese, Please!
Long a and Long e Game

paint	freight	these	me
	say	beach	weight
neat	thief		snake
tape	keep	play	chief

More Cheese, Please! More Cheese, Please!
Long a and Long e Game

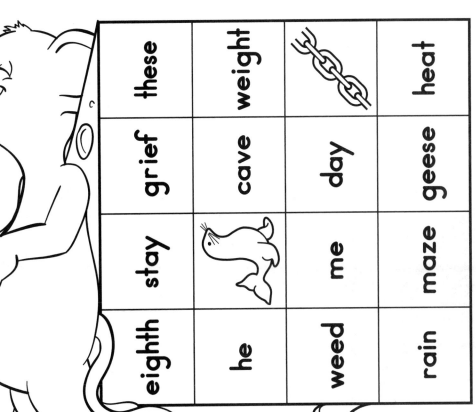

these	grief	stay	eighth
weight	cave		he
	day	me	weed
heat	geese	maze	rain

More Cheese, Please!
Long a and Long e Game

rain	chief	theme	tray
sleigh		speak	snake
geese	nail	wave	field
we	eight		neat

cave	flame	gate	maze	rake
TEC61063	TEC61063	TEC61063	TEC61063	TEC61063
shade	snake	tape	wave	chain
TEC61063	TEC61063	TEC61063	TEC61063	TEC61063
nail	paid	paint	rain	sail
TEC61063	TEC61063	TEC61063	TEC61063	TEC61063
tail	train	clay	day	hay
TEC61063	TEC61063	TEC61063	TEC61063	TEC61063
play	say	spray	stay	tray
TEC61063	TEC61063	TEC61063	TEC61063	TEC61063
eight	eighth	freight	sleigh	weight
TEC61063	TEC61063	TEC61063	TEC61063	TEC61063

he	me	she	we	eve
TEC61063	TEC61063	TEC61063	TEC61063	TEC61063
theme	these	scene	feet	geese
TEC61063	TEC61063	TEC61063	TEC61063	TEC61063
jeep	keep	knee	seed	sheep
TEC61063	TEC61063	TEC61063	TEC61063	TEC61063
weed	beach	bead	bean	heat
TEC61063	TEC61063	TEC61063	TEC61063	TEC61063
leaf	neat	seal	speak	brief
TEC61063	TEC61063	TEC61063	TEC61063	TEC61063
chief	field	grief	piece	thief
TEC61063	TEC61063	TEC61063	TEC61063	TEC61063

Go Hide!
Long *i* and Long *o* Game

What you need:
- gameboard copy (pages 13–15) for each player
- game markers, such as ¾" construction paper squares
- copy of the reproducible teacher cards (pages 16 and 17), cut apart, shuffled, and placed in an envelope

Directions:

1. Give game markers and a gameboard to each child. Have him read each word and name each picture on his board, noting the different spellings of long /i/ and long /o/. Provide assistance as necessary.

2. Explain that when a student hears a word that is written or pictured on his board, he is to cover it with a marker.

3. Describe the criteria for winning: four in a row (vertically, horizontally, or diagonally) or four corners. Ask that winners say, "Gotcha!" to signal their wins.

4. To play, remove a card from the envelope and read it aloud. (As you use the cards, place them faceup in alphabetical order for your later reference.) Students who have the matching word or picture cover it.

5. Play continues until someone calls out, "Gotcha!" To verify his win, have him uncover and read or name each word or picture as you check his responses. For an added challenge, have him spell any pictured word that he uncovers.

See page 67 for a student assessment page.

Go Hide!
Long *i* and Long *o* Game

find	dry	sold	crow
cold	(goat)	lie	hive
toe	vote	sky	tried
might	throw	(slide)	road

©The Mailbox® • *Phenomenal Phonics*® *Games* • TEC61063

Go Hide!
Long *i* and Long *o* Game

boat	smoke	nose	(kite)
grow	mice	sold	child
why	(bowl)	right	goal
fries	dime	kind	doe

©The Mailbox® • *Phenomenal Phonics*® *Games* • TEC61063

Go Hide!
Long *i* and Long *o* Game

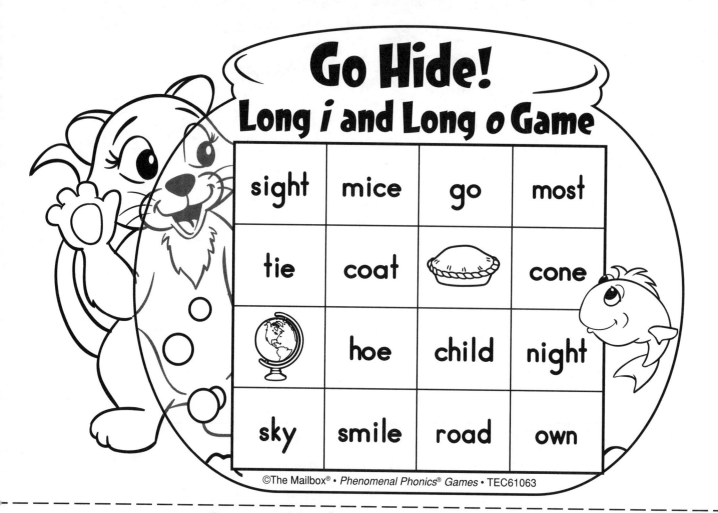

sight	mice	go	most
tie	coat	(pie)	cone
(globe)	hoe	child	night
sky	smile	road	own

©The Mailbox® • *Phenomenal Phonics*® Games • TEC61063

Go Hide!
Long *i* and Long *o* Game

nose	mind	tire	goes
(slate)	fly	dime	most
tried	both	glow	might
wild	toast	toe	(fries)

14   ©The Mailbox® • *Phenomenal Phonics*® Games • TEC61063

Go Hide!
Long *i* and Long *o* Game

hive	hoe		tie
find	toast	why	cold
smoke	night	grow	mind
	my	coat	drove

Go Hide!
Long *i* and Long *o* Game

	doe	both	my
sight	kind	throw	drove
crow	tire	go	wild
goal		lie	smile

child	find	kind	mind	wild
TEC61063	TEC61063	TEC61063	TEC61063	TEC61063
dime	hive	kite	mice	slide
TEC61063	TEC61063	TEC61063	TEC61063	TEC61063
smile	tire	cry	dry	fly
TEC61063	TEC61063	TEC61063	TEC61063	TEC61063
fry	my	sky	why	fries
TEC61063	TEC61063	TEC61063	TEC61063	TEC61063
lie	pie	tie	tried	light
TEC61063	TEC61063	TEC61063	TEC61063	TEC61063
might	night	right	sight	both
TEC61063	TEC61063	TEC61063	TEC61063	TEC61063

cold	comb	go	most	
TEC61063	TEC61063	TEC61063	TEC61063	
sold	bone	cone	drove	globe
TEC61063	TEC61063	TEC61063	TEC61063	TEC61063
nose	smoke	vote	boat	coat
TEC61063	TEC61063	TEC61063	TEC61063	TEC61063
goal	goat	road	soap	toast
TEC61063	TEC61063	TEC61063	TEC61063	TEC61063
bowl	crow	glow	grow	own
TEC61063	TEC61063	TEC61063	TEC61063	TEC61063
throw	doe	goes	hoe	toe
TEC61063	TEC61063	TEC61063	TEC61063	TEC61063

Swinging in the Shade
Long a and Long u Game

What you need:
- gameboard copy (pages 19–21) for each player
- game markers, such as ¾" construction paper squares
- copy of the reproducible teacher cards (pages 22 and 23), cut apart, shuffled, and placed in an envelope

Directions:

1. Give game markers and a gameboard to each child. Have her read each word and name each picture on her board, noting the different spellings of long /a/ and long /u/. Provide assistance as necessary.

2. Explain that when a student hears a word that is written or pictured on her board, she is to cover it with a marker.

3. Describe the criteria for winning: four in a row (vertically, horizontally, or diagonally) or four corners. Ask that winners say, "Whee!" to signal their wins.

4. To play, remove a card from the envelope and read it aloud. (As you use the cards, place them faceup in alphabetical order for your later reference.) Students who have the matching word or picture cover it.

5. Play continues until someone calls out, "Whee!" To verify her win, have her uncover and read or name each word or picture as you check her responses. For an added challenge, have her spell any pictured word that she uncovers.

See page 68 for a student assessment page.

Swinging in the Shade
Long a and Long u Game

flame	bugle	fuel	rail
	cube	amuse	gray
fume	trail	whale	music
pew	cave	pail	

Swinging in the Shade
Long a and Long u Game

tail	fuse	trade	bay
mew		mute	face
hay	music	name	pupil
cute	wait		fuel

cage	cave	crane	face	flame
TEC61063	TEC61063	TEC61063	TEC61063	TEC61063
gate	grapes	lake	name	tape
TEC61063	TEC61063	TEC61063	TEC61063	TEC61063
trade	whale	braid	grain	maid
TEC61063	TEC61063	TEC61063	TEC61063	TEC61063
mail	pail	rail	rain	tail
TEC61063	TEC61063	TEC61063	TEC61063	TEC61063
trail	wait	bay	day	gray
TEC61063	TEC61063	TEC61063	TEC61063	TEC61063

hay	may	play	stay	X-ray
TEC61063	TEC61063	TEC61063	TEC61063	TEC61063
bugle	cupid	fuel	human	music
TEC61063	TEC61063	TEC61063	TEC61063	TEC61063
pupil	unit	amuse	cube	cute
TEC61063	TEC61063	TEC61063	TEC61063	TEC61063
fume	fuse	huge	mule	muse
TEC61063	TEC61063	TEC61063	TEC61063	TEC61063
mute	use	few	mew	pew
TEC61063	TEC61063	TEC61063	TEC61063	TEC61063

Artwork by Ernie
R-Controlled Vowel Game

What you need:

- gameboard copy (pages 25–27) for each player

- game markers, such as ¾" construction paper squares

- copy of the reproducible teacher cards (pages 28 and 29), cut apart, shuffled, and placed in an envelope

Directions:

1. Give game markers and a gameboard to each child. Have her read each word and name each picture on her board, noting the different *r*-controlled vowels. Provide assistance as necessary.

2. Explain that when a student hears a word that is written or pictured on her board, she is to cover it with a marker.

3. Describe the criteria for winning: four in a row (vertically, horizontally, or diagonally) or four corners. Ask that winners say, "Ernie's art!" to signal their wins.

4. To play, remove a card from the envelope and read it aloud. (As you use the cards, place them faceup in alphabetical order for your later reference.) Students who have the matching word or picture cover it.

5. Play continues until someone calls out, "Ernie's art!" To verify her win, have her uncover and read or name each word or picture as you check her responses. For an added challenge, have her spell any pictured word that she uncovers.

See page 70 for a student assessment page.

Artwork by Ernie
R-Controlled Vowel Game

swirl	fern	turtle	term
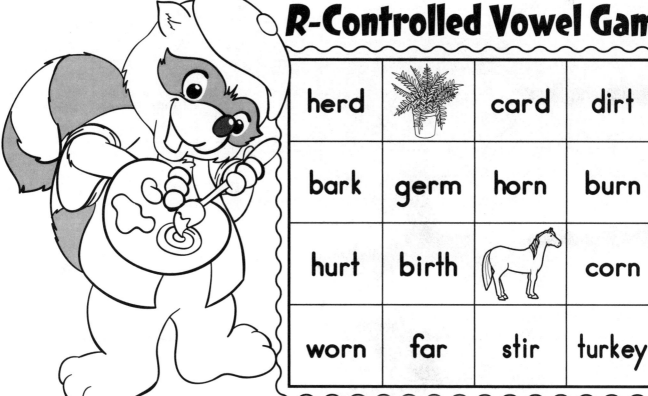	curl	arm	girl
circle	pork	her	born
star	fort		blurt

Artwork by Ernie
R-Controlled Vowel Game

herd		card	dirt
bark	germ	horn	burn
hurt	birth		corn
worn	far	stir	turkey

Artwork by Ernie
R-Controlled Vowel Game

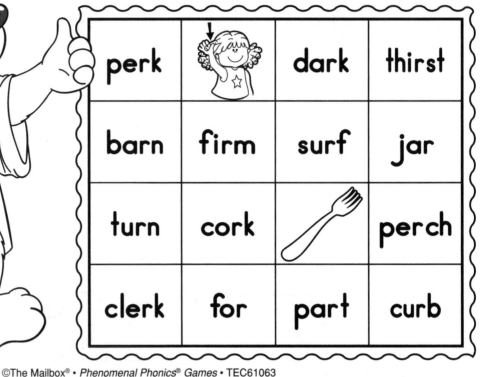

perk		dark	thirst
barn	firm	surf	jar
turn	cork		perch
clerk	for	part	curb

Artwork by Ernie
R-Controlled Vowel Game

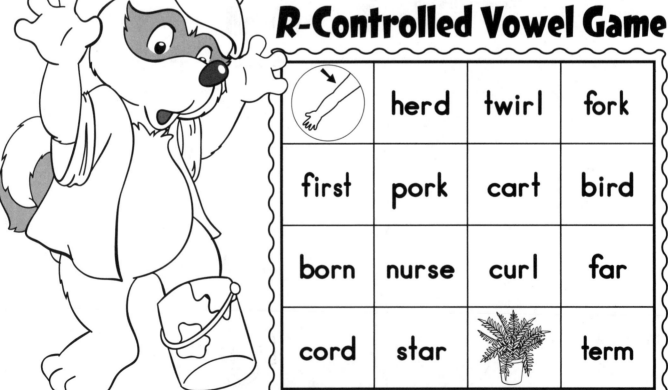

	herd	twirl	fork
first	pork	cart	bird
born	nurse	curl	far
cord	star		term

Artwork by Ernie
R-Controlled Vowel Game

shirt	car	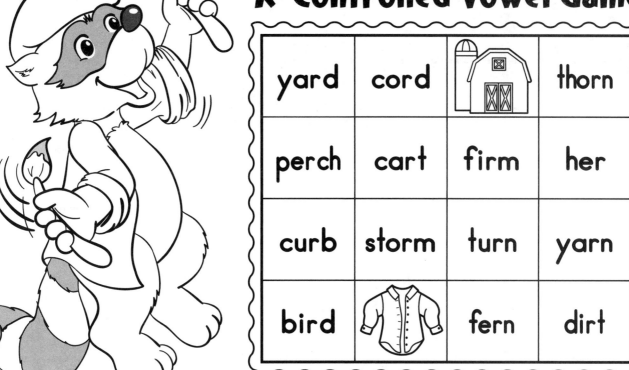	surf
for	purse	north	girl
bark	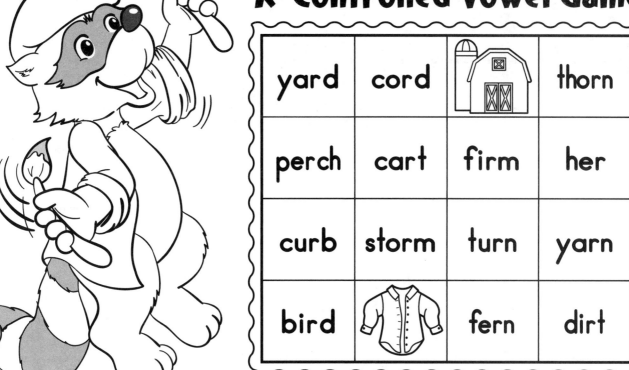	germ	perk
third	dark	burn	part

Artwork by Ernie
R-Controlled Vowel Game

yard	cord	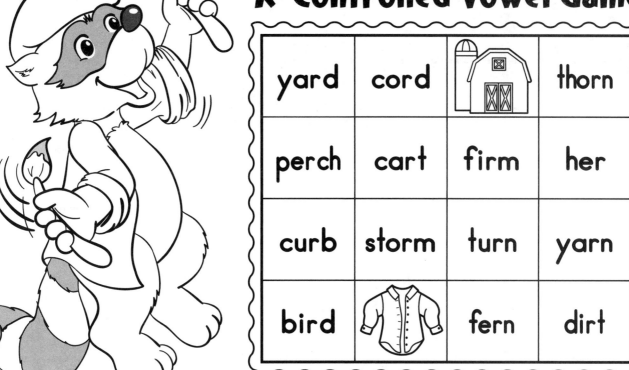	thorn
perch	cart	firm	her
curb	storm	turn	yarn
bird	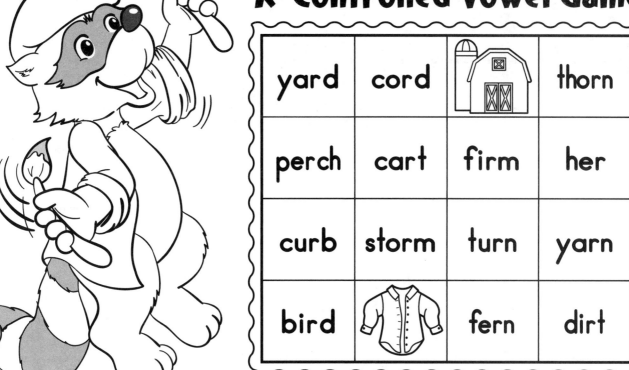	fern	dirt

Reproducible Teacher Cards
Use with the directions on page 24.

arm	bark	barn	car	card
TEC61063	TEC61063	TEC61063	TEC61063	TEC61063
cart	dark	far	jar	part
TEC61063	TEC61063	TEC61063	TEC61063	TEC61063
star	yard	yarn	clerk	fern
TEC61063	TEC61063	TEC61063	TEC61063	TEC61063
germ	her	herd	perch	perk
TEC61063	TEC61063	TEC61063	TEC61063	TEC61063
term	bird	birth	circle	dirt
TEC61063	TEC61063	TEC61063	TEC61063	TEC61063
firm	first	girl	shirt	stir
TEC61063	TEC61063	TEC61063	TEC61063	TEC61063

swirl	third	thirst	twirl	born
TEC61063	TEC61063	TEC61063	TEC61063	TEC61063
cord	cork	corn	for	fork
TEC61063	TEC61063	TEC61063	TEC61063	TEC61063
fort	horn	horse	north	pork
TEC61063	TEC61063	TEC61063	TEC61063	TEC61063
storm	thorn	worn	blurt	burn
TEC61063	TEC61063	TEC61063	TEC61063	TEC61063
curb	curl	hurt	nurse	purse
TEC61063	TEC61063	TEC61063	TEC61063	TEC61063
surf	turkey	turn	turtle	
TEC61063	TEC61063	TEC61063	TEC61063	

Clown's House
Diphthongs ou and ow Game

See page 71 for a student assessment page.

What you need:
- gameboard copy (pages 31–33) for each player
- game markers, such as ¾" construction paper squares
- copy of the reproducible teacher cards (pages 34 and 35), cut apart, shuffled, and placed in an envelope

Directions:

1. Give game markers and a gameboard to each child. Have him read each word and name each picture on his board, noting the similar sounds of the diphthongs *ou* and *ow*. Provide assistance as necessary.

2. Explain that when a student hears a word that is written or pictured on his board, he is to cover it with a marker.

3. Describe the criteria for winning: four in a row (vertically, horizontally, or diagonally) or four corners. Ask that winners say, "Howdy, clown!" to signal their wins.

4. To play, remove a card from the envelope and read it aloud. (As you use the cards, place them faceup in alphabetical order for your later reference.) Students who have the matching word or picture cover it.

5. Play continues until someone calls out, "Howdy, clown!" To verify his win, have him uncover and read or name each word or picture as you check his responses. For an added challenge, have him spell any pictured word that he uncovers.

Clown's House
Diphthongs ou and ow Game

now	mount	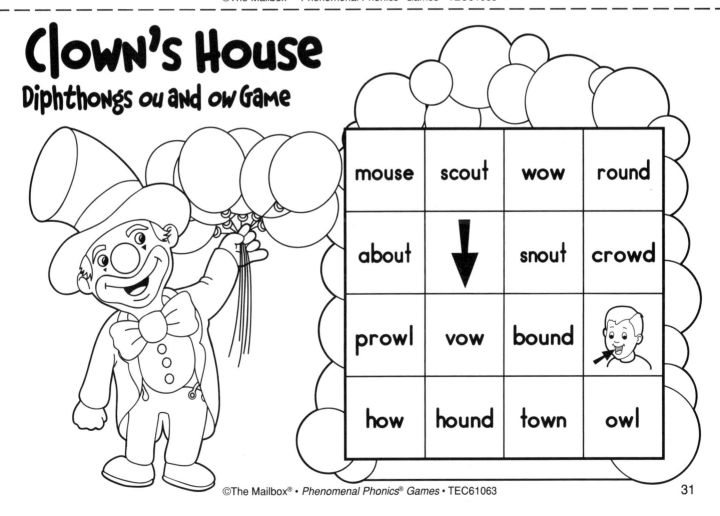	ground
hound	prowl	down	count
clown		shout	gown
brown	pow	proud	out

Clown's House
Diphthongs ou and ow Game

mouse	scout	wow	round
about	↓	snout	crowd
prowl	vow	bound	
how	hound	town	owl

Clown's House
Diphthongs *ou* and *ow* Game

gown	now	ouch	
crown	count	how	found
loud	🦉	round	drown
proud	sound	plow	scowl

©The Mailbox® • *Phenomenal Phonics*® *Games* • TEC61063

Clown's House
Diphthongs *ou* and *ow* Game

ounce	scowl	🐭	pow
crowd	fowl	stout	pouch
mound	about	cow	howl
👑	out	growl	loud

©The Mailbox® • *Phenomenal Phonics*® *Games* • TEC61063

Clown's House
Diphthongs *ou* and *ow* Game

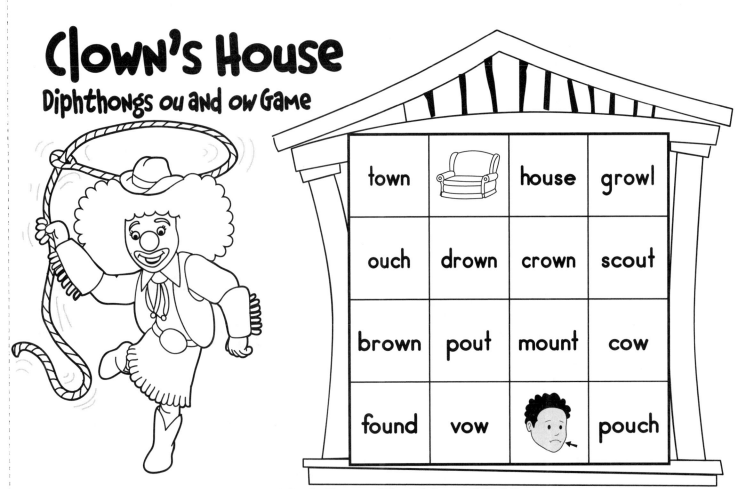

town		house	growl
ouch	drown	crown	scout
brown	pout	mount	cow
found	vow		pouch

Clown's House
Diphthongs *ou* and *ow* Game

wow	pound	gown	frown
	town	count	plow
snout	howl		ounce
couch	mouth	fowl	sound

33

Reproducible Teacher Cards
Use with the directions on page 30.

about	bounce	bound	cloud	couch
count	found	ground	hound	house
loud	mound	mount	mouse	mouth
ouch	ounce	out	pouch	pound
pout	proud	round	scout	shout

snout	sound	stout	brown	clown
TEC61063	TEC61063	TEC61063	TEC61063	TEC61063
cow	crowd	crown	down	drown
TEC61063	TEC61063	TEC61063	TEC61063	TEC61063
fowl	frown	gown	growl	how
TEC61063	TEC61063	TEC61063	TEC61063	TEC61063
howl	now	owl	plow	pow
TEC61063	TEC61063	TEC61063	TEC61063	TEC61063
prowl	scowl	town	vow	wow
TEC61063	TEC61063	TEC61063	TEC61063	TEC61063

Oh Boy, Toys!
Diphthongs *oi* and *oy* Game

What you need:
- gameboard copy (pages 37–39) for each player
- game markers, such as ¾" construction paper squares
- copy of the reproducible teacher cards (pages 40 and 41), cut apart, shuffled, and placed in an envelope

Directions:

1. Give game markers and a gameboard to each child. Have her read each word and name each picture on her board, noting the similar sounds of the diphthongs *oi* and *oy*. Provide assistance as necessary.

2. Explain that when a student hears a word that is written or pictured on her board, she is to cover it with a marker.

3. Describe the criteria for winning: four in a row (vertically, horizontally, or diagonally) or four corners. Ask that winners say, "Woof!" to signal their wins.

4. To play, remove a card from the envelope and read it aloud. (As you use the cards, place them faceup in alphabetical order for your later reference.) Students who have the matching word or picture cover it.

5. Play continues until someone calls out, "Woof!" To verify her win, have her uncover and read or name each word or picture as you check her responses. For an added challenge, have her spell any pictured word that she uncovers.

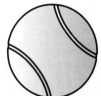

See page 72 for a student assessment page.

Oh Boy, Toys!
Diphthongs *oi* and *oy* Game

enjoy	coy	choice	join
decoy	coil		foil
boil	joy	noise	ploy
spoil		destroy annoy	

Oh Boy, Toys!
Diphthongs *oi* and *oy* Game

joint	cowboy	ahoy
soy	foil	royal
boy	choice	oil
coy	employ	soil hoist
voice		

Oh Boy, Toys!
Diphthongs *oi* and *oy* Game

coin	ploy	annoy	moist
	enjoy	boys	boiler
royal	foil	hoist	employ
soy	poise	join	

Oh Boy, Toys!
Diphthongs *oi* and *oy* Game

loyal	noise		voice
void	point	ahoy	toys
joy		joyful	join
broil	soy	boiler	ploy

38

Oh Boy, Toys!
Diphthongs *oi* and *oy* Game

decoy	spoil	toil	toy
	voice	destroy	noise
boys	employ	coin	
joint	loyal	joyful	coil

©The Mailbox® • Phenomenal Phonics® Games • TEC61063

Oh Boy, Toys!
Diphthongs *oi* and *oy* Game

destroy	coin	ahoy	point
enjoy	poise		toy
broil	royal	joy	toil
joyful		moist	void

©The Mailbox® • Phenomenal Phonics® Games • TEC61063

39

Reproducible Teacher Cards
Use with the directions on page 36.

boil TEC61063	**boiler** TEC61063	**broil** TEC61063	**choice** TEC61063
coil TEC61063	**coin** TEC61063	**foil** TEC61063	**hoist** TEC61063
join TEC61063	**joint** TEC61063	**moist** TEC61063	**noise** TEC61063
oil TEC61063	**point** TEC61063	**poise** TEC61063	**soil** TEC61063
spoil TEC61063	**toil** TEC61063	**voice** TEC61063	**void** TEC61063

ahoy	annoy	boy	boys
cowboy	coy	decoy	destroy
employ	enjoy	joy	joyful
loyal	ploy	royal	soy
toy	toys		

Rootin'-Tootin' Wrangler Silent Beginning-Letter Game

gn, kn, wr

What you need:

- gameboard copy (pages 43–45) for each player

- game markers, such as ¾" construction paper squares

- copy of the reproducible teacher cards (pages 46 and 47), cut apart, shuffled, and placed in an envelope

Directions:

1. Give game markers and a gameboard to each child. Have him read each word and name each picture on his board, noting the different silent beginning consonants. Provide assistance as necessary.

2. Explain that when a student hears a word that is written or pictured on his board, he is to cover it with a marker.

3. Describe the criteria for winning: four in a row (vertically, horizontally, or diagonally) or four corners. Ask that winners say, "Yee-haw!" to signal their wins.

4. To play, remove a card from the envelope and read it aloud. (As you use the cards, place them faceup in alphabetical order for your later reference.) Students who have the matching word or picture cover it.

5. Play continues until someone calls out, "Yee-haw!" To verify his win, have him uncover and read or name each word or picture as you check his responses. For an added challenge, have him spell any pictured word that he uncovers.

See page 74 for a student assessment page.

Rootin'-Tootin' Wrangler
Silent Beginning-Letter Game

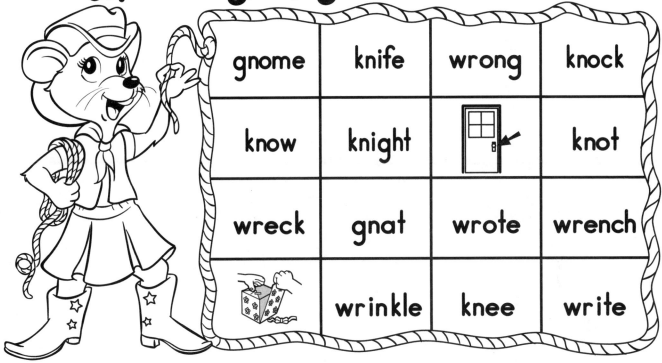

gnome	knife	wrong	knock
know	knight		knot
wreck	gnat	wrote	wrench
	wrinkle	knee	write

Rootin'-Tootin' Wrangler
Silent Beginning-Letter Game

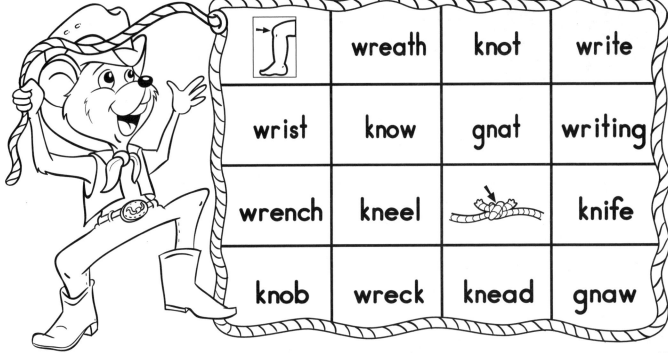

	wreath	knot	write
wrist	know	gnat	writing
wrench	kneel		knife
knob	wreck	knead	gnaw

Rootin'-Tootin' Wrangler
Silent Beginning-Letter Game

knight	wrong		knot
kneel	gnaw	knit	knew
	knuckle	wrap	wrote
knack	wrinkle	know	gnome

Rootin'-Tootin' Wrangler
Silent Beginning-Letter Game

wrist	knew	wrong	knight
knead		writing	gnat
wreath	wreck	knock	gnome
knit	knee	gnaw	

Rootin'-Tootin' Wrangler
Silent Beginning-Letter Game

	wrote	knob	gnome
gnat	knuckle	knew	wreck
kneel	knight	wrist	knead
wrinkle	knack		know

Rootin'-Tootin' Wrangler
Silent Beginning-Letter Game

writing	gnaw	wrench	knack
	knead	wrote	kneel
knit	knife		knot
wrap	knuckle	gnat	know

Reproducible Teacher Cards
Use with the directions on page 42.

gnat TEC61063	gnaw TEC61063	gnome TEC61063
knack TEC61063	knead TEC61063	knee TEC61063
kneel TEC61063	knew TEC61063	knife TEC61063
knight TEC61063	knit TEC61063	knob TEC61063
knock TEC61063	knot TEC61063	know TEC61063

knuckle TEC61063	wrap TEC61063	wreath TEC61063
wreck TEC61063	wrench TEC61063	wrinkle TEC61063
wrist TEC61063	write TEC61063	writing TEC61063
wrong TEC61063	wrote TEC61063	

Strike It Rich
Three-Letter Blend Game

What you need:

• gameboard copy (pages 49–51) for each player

• game markers, such as ¾" construction paper squares

• copy of the reproducible teacher cards (pages 52 and 53), cut apart, shuffled, and placed in an envelope

Directions:

1. Give game markers and a gameboard to each child. Have her read each word and name each picture on her board, noting the different blends. Provide assistance as necessary.

2. Explain that when a student hears a word that is written or pictured on her board, she is to cover it with a marker.

3. Describe the criteria for winning: four in a row (vertically, horizontally, or diagonally) or four corners. Ask that winners say, "Strike it rich!" to signal their wins.

4. To play, remove a card from the envelope and read it aloud. (As you use the cards, place them faceup in alphabetical order for your later reference.) Students who have the matching word or picture cover it.

5. Play continues until someone calls out, "Strike it rich!" To verify her win, have her uncover and read or name each word or picture as you check her responses. For an added challenge, have her spell any pictured word that she uncovers.

See page 75 for a student assessment page.

Strike It Rich
Three-Letter Blend Game

scratch	sprint	strand	🔺
threw	thrill	shrine	shriek
string	3	strong	scrap
shrub	sprout	scroll	spree

Strike It Rich
Three-Letter Blend Game

🧵	stripe	throb	shrug
scrub	shrink	street	screech
throw	sprain	script	steam
spruce	🔩	strut	shred

Strike It Rich
Three-Letter Blend Game

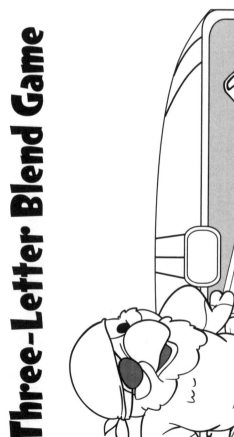

shrub	scram	throat	
thrifty	screw	sprint	strap
sprain	shrimp	stroke	throne
spread		scream	shrunk

Strike It Rich
Three-Letter Blend Game

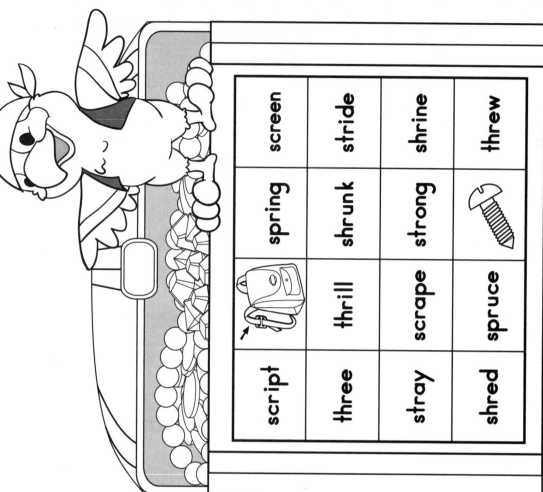

script	spring	screen
three	thrill	shrunk	stride
stray	scrape	strong	shrine
shred	spruce		threw

Strike It Rich
Three-Letter Blend Game

strut	spree		sprint
3	scroll	scream	throb
sprout	throat	thrifty	stroke
stray	shrimp	shred	scrub

Strike It Rich
Three-Letter Blend Game

street	shrimp	throne	scram
spread		spring	stream
throw	scratch	shrink	
stripe	shrug	thrill	scrap

Reproducible Teacher Cards
Use with the directions on page 48.

scream TEC61063	scroll TEC61063	shrine TEC61063	sprain TEC61063	sprint TEC61063
scratch TEC61063	script TEC61063	shrimp TEC61063	shrunk TEC61063	spring TEC61063
scrape TEC61063	screw TEC61063	shriek TEC61063	shrug TEC61063	spree TEC61063
scrap TEC61063	screen TEC61063	shred TEC61063	shrub TEC61063	spread TEC61063
scram TEC61063	screech TEC61063	scrub TEC61063	shrink TEC61063	spray TEC61063

©The Mailbox® • *Phenomenal Phonics*® *Games* • TEC61063

straw TEC61063	string TEC61063	thread TEC61063	throat TEC61063	throw TEC61063
strap TEC61063	stride TEC61063	strut TEC61063	thrill TEC61063	throne TEC61063
strand TEC61063	street TEC61063	strong TEC61063	thrifty TEC61063	throb TEC61063
spruce TEC61063	stream TEC61063	stroke TEC61063	threw TEC61063	
sprout TEC61063	stray TEC61063	stripe TEC61063	three TEC61063	

Beach Buddies Plural Ending Game

What you need:
- gameboard copy (pages 55–57) for each player
- game markers, such as ¾" construction paper squares
- copy of the reproducible teacher cards (pages 58 and 59), cut apart, shuffled, and placed in an envelope

Directions:

1. Give game markers and a gameboard to each child. Have him read each word and name each picture on his board, noting the different plural endings. Provide assistance as necessary.

2. Explain that if a student hears a word whose plural spelling is written on his board, he is to cover the corresponding word with a marker.

3. Describe the criteria for winning: four in a row (vertically, horizontally, or diagonally) or four corners. Ask that winners say, "Beach buddies!" to signal their wins.

4. To play, remove a card from the envelope and read it aloud. (As you use the cards, place them faceup in alphabetical order for your later reference.) Students who have the matching word or picture cover it.

5. Play continues until someone calls out, "Beach buddies!" To verify his win, have him uncover and read each word as you check his responses. For an added challenge, have him say the rule used to form each plural word.

See page 76 for a student assessment page.

Beach Buddies
Plural Ending Game

dresses	berries	towels	lunches
snacks	flies	pencils	sixes
shovels	desks	benches	candies
bushes	ladies	cars	classes

Beach Buddies
Plural Ending Game

lunches	pencils	fries	dishes
cities	carrots	dresses	berries
crabs	toys	peaches	frogs
bosses	bunnies	daisies	foxes

Beach Buddies
Plural Ending Game

glasses	ducks	cars	fries
dishes	puppies	bosses	hats
ladies	daisies	berries	beaches
boxes	crabs	classes	snacks

Beach Buddies
Plural Ending Game

carrots	puppies	dresses	babies
buckets	lunches	bunnies	candies
drinks	boxes	toys	glasses
peaches	benches	ladies	shells

Beach Buddies
Plural Ending Game

sixes	buckets	puppies	couches
flies	cities	drinks	bunnies
glasses	ducks	benches	flashes
crabs	towels	hats	daisies

Beach Buddies
Plural Ending Game

peaches	shelves	desks	flashes
shells	cars	boxes	candies
cities	beaches	pencils	fries
babies	foxes	frogs	bushes

Reproducible Teacher Cards

Use with the directions on page 54.

beach TEC61063	**bench** TEC61063	**boss** TEC61063	**box** TEC61063
bush TEC61063	**class** TEC61063	**couch** TEC61063	**dish** TEC61063
dress TEC61063	**flash** TEC61063	**fox** TEC61063	**glass** TEC61063
lunch TEC61063	**peach** TEC61063	**six** TEC61063	**baby** TEC61063
berry TEC61063	**bunny** TEC61063	**candy** TEC61063	**city** TEC61063

©The Mailbox® • *Phenomenal Phonics® Games* • TEC61063

daisy	fly	fry	lady
TEC61063	TEC61063	TEC61063	TEC61063
puppy	bucket	car	carrot
TEC61063	TEC61063	TEC61063	TEC61063
crab	desk	drink	duck
TEC61063	TEC61063	TEC61063	TEC61063
frog	hat	pencil	snack
TEC61063	TEC61063	TEC61063	TEC61063
shell	shovel	towel	toy
TEC61063	TEC61063	TEC61063	TEC61063

Can't Catch Us!
Contraction Game

What you need:
- gameboard copy (pages 61–63) for each player
- game markers, such as ¾" construction paper squares
- copy of the reproducible teacher cards (pages 64 and 65), cut apart, shuffled, and placed in an envelope

Directions:

1. Give game markers and a gameboard to each child. Have her read each word and name each picture on her board, noting the different contractions. Provide assistance as necessary.

2. Explain that if a student hears a word pair that matches a contraction written on her board, she is to cover the contraction with a marker.

3. Describe the criteria for winning: four in a row (vertically, horizontally, or diagonally) or four corners. Ask that winners say, "Ribbit!" to signal their wins.

4. To play, remove a card from the envelope and read the word pair aloud. (Place the card faceup for your later reference.) Students who have the corresponding contraction cover it.

5. Play continues until someone calls out, "Ribbit!" To verify her win, have her uncover and read each contraction as you check her responses. For an added challenge, have her say the two words that make each contraction.

See page 77 for a student assessment page.

Can't Catch Us!
Contraction Game

can't	they've	wasn't	it's
he'll	I'm	you're	won't
that's	weren't	hasn't	he's
aren't	doesn't	we'll	shouldn't

Can't Catch Us!
Contraction Game

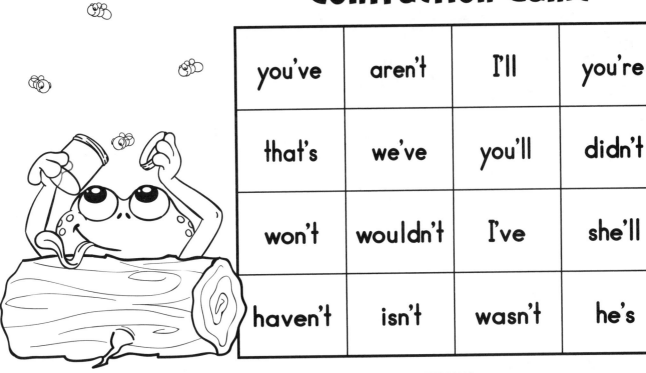

you've	aren't	I'll	you're
that's	we've	you'll	didn't
won't	wouldn't	I've	she'll
haven't	isn't	wasn't	he's

Can't Catch Us!
Contraction Game

they'll	you're	didn't	I'm
hadn't	we've	he'll	it'll
I've	can't	that's	weren't
shouldn't	we're	isn't	don't

Can't Catch Us!
Contraction Game

it'll	don't	they're	won't
doesn't	I've	wasn't	couldn't
she's	he'll	it's	shouldn't
isn't	hasn't	we've	you'll

Can't Catch Us!
Contraction Game

couldn't	she's	isn't	doesn't
I'll	we're	she'll	you've
wouldn't	aren't	don't	we'll
they've	hadn't	I'm	can't

Can't Catch Us!
Contraction Game

didn't	weren't	they'll	we'll
wouldn't	it's	haven't	he's
it'll	you've	wasn't	couldn't
we're	hadn't	you'll	they're

I am	they are	we are
TEC61063	TEC61063	TEC61063
you are	I have	they have
TEC61063	TEC61063	TEC61063
we have	you have	he is
TEC61063	TEC61063	TEC61063
are not	can not	could not
TEC61063	TEC61063	TEC61063
did not	do not	does not
TEC61063	TEC61063	TEC61063

had not TEC61063	has not TEC61063	have not TEC61063
is not TEC61063	was not TEC61063	were not TEC61063
will not TEC61063	would not TEC61063	should not TEC61063
he will TEC61063	I will TEC61063	it will TEC61063
she will TEC61063	they will TEC61063	we will TEC61063
you will TEC61063		

More Cheese, Please!

Circle each correct spelling.

Write each word.

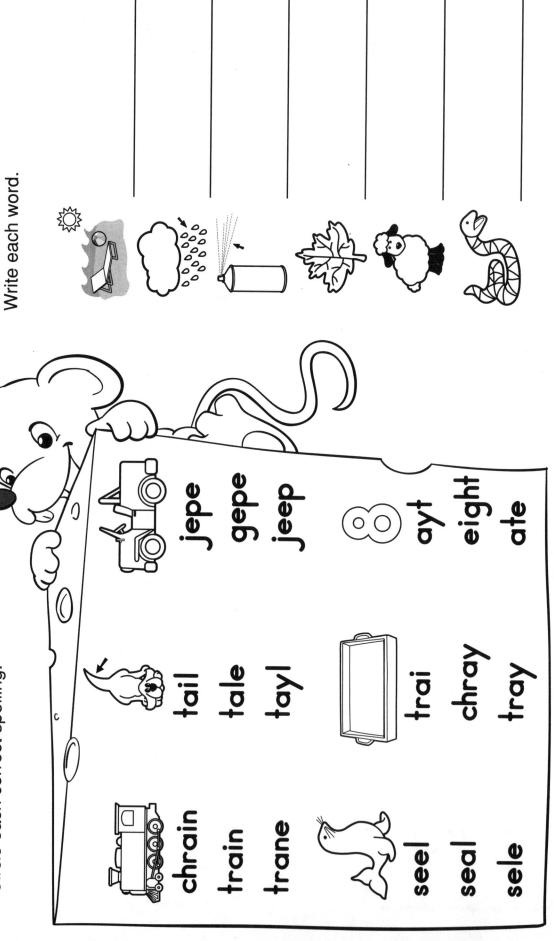

chrain
train
trane

seel
seal
sele

tail
tale
tayl

trai
chray
tray

jepe
gepe
jeep

ayt
eight
ate

Note to the teacher: Use with the directions on page 6.

Go Hide!

Circle each correct spelling.

Write each word.

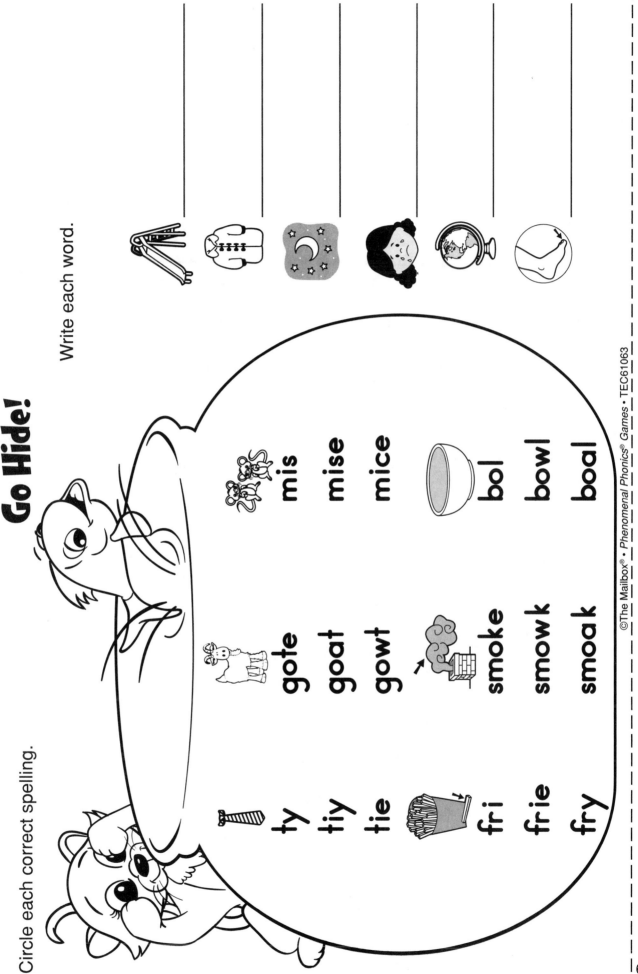

mis
mise
mice

bol
bowl
boal

gote
goat
gowt

smoke
smowk
smoak

ty
tiy
tie

fri
frie
fry

Note to the teacher: Use with the directions on page 12.

Name _____

Swinging in the Shade

Circle the correct word for each picture.

gait
gate
gayt

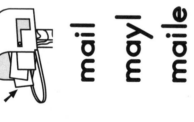

cewpid
cuepid
cupid

mail
mayl
maile

byugle
buegle
bugle

whail
whale
wayl

rane
rain
rayn

Write each word.

_____

_____

_____

_____

_____

_____

Note to the teacher: Use with the directions on page 18.

68

A Long-Vowel Celebration

Circle the correct spelling.

jeyp	graips	hive	myl	glowb
jeep	grayps	highv	mule	gloeb
gepe	grapes	hyv	mewl	globe

Write the word.

1. _____

2. _____

3. _____

4. _____

5. _____

6. _____

7. _____

8. _____

9. _____

10. _____

Note to the teacher: Use after completing the games described on pages 6, 12, and 18.

Artwork by Ernie

Write each word.

Circle the correct spelling for each picture.

turtle
turtle
tartle

thorn
thurn
tharn

fern
firn
furn

bard
bird
bord

parse
purse
porse

yern
yorn
yarn

Note to the teacher: Use with the directions on page 24.

Assessment of diphthongs *ou* and *ow* spellings

Clown's House

Circle each correct spelling.

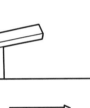

cloun
clown
klown

awll
owl
owll

down
downe
doune

bounce
bounse
bownce

mowth
mowf
mouth

hous
house
howse

Write each word.

_____

_____

_____

_____

_____

_____

©The Mailbox® • *Phenomenal Phonics® Games* • TEC61063

Note to the teacher: Use with the directions on page 30.

71

Oh Boy, Toys!

Circle each correct spelling.

Write each word.

soil
soile
soyle

bois
boys
boyes

toise
toyes
toys

boyl
boil
boile

Note to the teacher: Use with the directions on page 36.

A Diphthong Celebration

Circle the correct spelling.

mowse	frown	coyn	bouys
moyse	froun	coin	bois
mouse	froin	cown	boys

Write the word.

1. _____

2. _____

3.  _____

4.  _____

5.  _____

6.  _____

7.  _____

8.  _____

9. _____

10. _____

©The Mailbox® • Phenomenal Phonics® Games • TEC61063

Note to the teacher: Use after completing the games described on pages 30 and 36.

73

Assessment of silent beginning letters

Rootin'-Tootin' Wrangler

Use a blend from the box to complete each word.

| gn | kn | wr |

_____ee

_____aw

_____at

_____ong

_____ite

_____ob

Circle the correct spelling for each word.

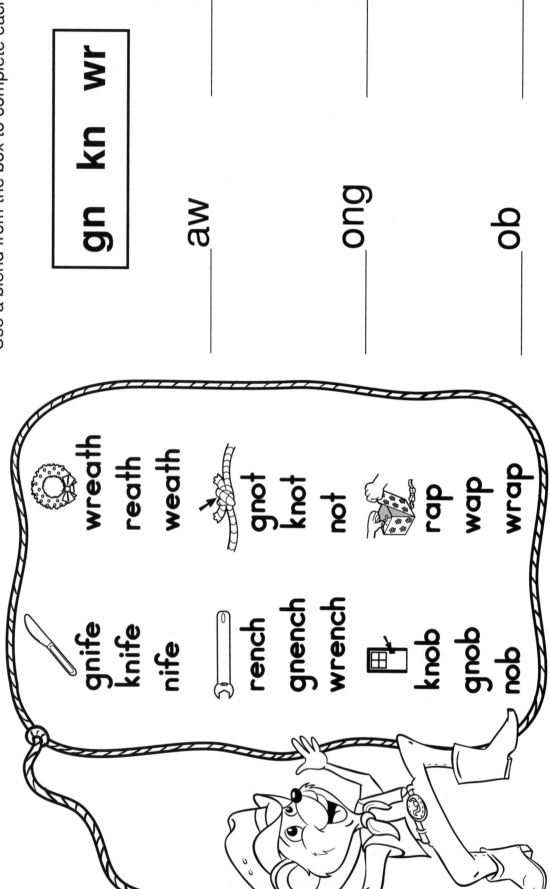

wreath
reath
weath

gnife
knife
nife

gnot
knot
not

rench
gnench
wrench

rap
wap
wrap

knob
gnob
nob

©The Mailbox® • Phenomenal Phonics® Games • TEC61063

Note to the teacher: Use with the directions on page 42.

Strike It Rich

Circle the correct spelling
for each picture.

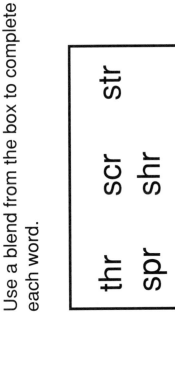

screw
strew
skrew

thee
tree
three

sray
spray
shray

shraw
straw
scraw

Use a blend from the box to complete
each word.

thr	scr	str
spr	shr	

_____oke   _____een

_____ape   _____int

_____ink   _____one

Note to the teacher: Use with the directions on page 48.

Beach Buddies

Circle the correct plural spelling for each word.

fly	**dish**	**couch**
flies	dishs	couchies
flyes	dishes	couchs
flys	dishies	couches

pencil	**six**
penciles	sixs
pencilies	sixes
pencils	sixies

Write the plural spelling of each word.

peach _____

baby _____

car _____

glass _____

berry _____

fox _____

©The Mailbox® • *Phenomenal Phonics® Games* • TEC61063

Note to the teacher: Use with the directions on page 54.

Can't Catch Us!

Circle the word pair that matches each contraction.

can't	**I'm**
can not	I are
can are	I am
can is	I is
it's	**they've**
it not	they not
it are	they have
it is	they is
you'll	**isn't**
you will	is are
you is	is am
you are	is not

Write each contraction.

he will _____

has not _____

we have _____

we are _____

that is _____

I have _____

did not _____

I will _____

77

Note to the teacher: Use with the directions on page 60.

Storage Labels

Copy and cut out the storage labels on pages 78–80. Glue each label to a large manila envelope. Then place copies of the corresponding student gameboards and teacher cards inside each envelope. If desired, store a copy of the teacher page, copies of the corresponding brag tags, and game markers in the envelopes as well.

Use with the games described on pages 6 and 12.

    ©The Mailbox® • *Phenomenal Phonics® Games* • TEC61063

Swinging in the Shade
Long *a* and Long *u* Game

TEC61063

Artwork by Ernie
R-Controlled Vowel Game

TEC61063

Clown's House
Diphthongs *ou* and *ow* Game

TEC61063

Oh Boy, Toys!
Diphthongs *oi* and *oy* Game

TEC61063

Storage Labels

Use with the games described on pages 42, 48, 54, and 60.

Rootin'-Tootin' Wrangler

Silent Beginning-
Letter Game:
gn, kn, wr

TEC61063

Strike It Rich

Three-Letter
Blend Game

TEC61063

BEACH BUDDIES

PLURAL
ENDING
GAME

TEC61063

Can't Catch Us!

Contraction Game

TEC61063